Daily Prayer Guide: Pray & Get Results Every Day.

Practical Step-by-Step Guide to Develop a Powerful Personal Prayer Life Despite Your Busy Schedules.

Daniel C. Okpara

Published By:
Better Life Media.
BETTER LIFE WORLD OUTREACH CENTER.
Website: www.BetterLifeWorld.org
Email: info@betterlifeworld.org

This title and others are available for quantity discounts for sale promotions, gifts and evangelism. Visit our website or email us to get started.

Any scripture quotation in this book is taken from the KJV except where stated. Used by permission.

All texts, calls, letters, testimonies and enquiries are welcome.

Dedication

To the Holy Spirit who helps me in prayer.

To Rev. David Nwolisa whose prayer life has influenced mine greatly.

To my wife, Doris, who has prayed every day for me.

To my mother, Louisa, for teaching me to do my first fasting early in life.

To you, reading this book. May you encounter God in your prayers going forward.

FREE BONUS ...

Download These Powerful Books Today for

FREE... And Take Your Relationship With

God to a New Level.

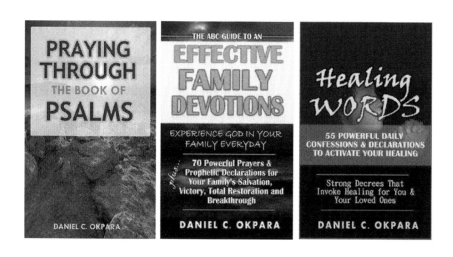

Go Here to Download:

www.betterlifeworld.org/grow

CONTENTS.

Introduction

"I know I should pray, but I can't.

"Why?"

"I could watch a movie for 4 hours or chat on social media for several hours at a stretch, without getting bored, but whenever you say, pray, I get sleepy. What's wrong with me?"

"Yes I know. I have heard a lot about the power of prayer. I have read a lot about great men of God who prayed and moved mountains. But I still can't pray, why, what's wrong with me?"

"Why is it that what I want to do is not what I

find myself doing?"

This was me years ago as I struggled to understand prayer and pray more. And I know this is also the state of several Christians today.

Yes. We know we should pray. They preach that to us every Sunday. But the question is, how do we pray? How do we really grow a rich praying life? How can we make prayer a part and parcel of our lives?

This was the question I kept asking myself several years ago; as I kept struggling with guilt, about not praying the way I should really do. Just like the disciples, I kept crying inside me, ***"LORD, teach me how to pray!"***

This book is an attempt to share with believers practical tips that God has shown me in my walk with Him, according to His Word, on how we can really pray more....and really get answers to our prayers.

Chapter 1: God Is Calling: Your Heart Is Beating: 10 Serious Reasons Why You Must Grow A Consistent Daily Prayer Life.

In order to deal with my own prayerlessness, the LORD laid it on my heart that if I don't have enough reasons to pray, that I would never want to pray. Everything we want to do in life begins with answering why do we want to do it. Until we can see enough **whys** we can't muster the courage to take the risks.

So in this chapter, let's look at the whys that God showed me to motivate me to start praying.

Someone said that *"prayer is the smallest of all acts, but the greatest of all forces".*

In our today's world, there are so many things that need our time. So many that prayers now become the most irrelevant of all of the things we should be worried about.

Some people are now even questioning whether prayer really does anything. I've read in places where people say that prayer simply makes the person praying to feel good. And that it doesn't really bring any meaningful changes in life.

Of course, this is the biggest of all the lies

Satan is using to blackmail people from praying. The truth is that prayer works. Prayer brings great changes. Prayer moves mountains. Prayer changes governments.

If we can spend 20% of the time we spend on social media and other things that don't matter on our prayer knees, we would have revival in the church so fast. Unfortunately, the more busy we are, and stay away from praying, the more we don't get closer to what we are chasing.

Why should we start praying?

1. God Commands Us To Pray.

The Bible says in the book of Luke 18:1:

And he spake a parable unto them [to this end], that men ought always to pray, and not to faint.

Then in 1 Thessalonians 5: 17 Paul puts it this way,

"Pray continually".

I see the admonition to pray as an express commandment, a commandment that disobeying it is equivalent to disobeying the commandment not to commit murder.

Why are we commanded to pray?

Jesus answered that when He said:

"Watch and pray, that ye enter not into temptation: the spirit indeed [is] willing, but the flesh [is] weak. **(Matthew 26:41)**

Jesus is simply saying that if you don't watch and pray as you should, you will fall into temptations regularly. Without an effective and consistent daily prayer life, you will open door for many other evil influences in your life.

2. Only Through Prayer Can God Have Access Into Your Life To Help You.

In the world we live today, there are many questions. Millions of people are asking, "But if God really owns the world, why doesn't he intervene in this and that situation?"

Beloved, let's quit accusing God for not helping us as He should have. We are creatures of choice. It is only when we call on God for help that He comes in to help. God doesn't barge into people's lives without their permission. It is only by a consistent prayer life that we create room for God into our lives, families and endeavors.

"Ask and it will be given to you; seek and you will find; knock and the door will be opened unto you." (Matt 7: 7)

Luke 18:6-7: And the Lord said, *"Listen to what the unjust judge says. And will not God bring about justice for his chosen ones, who cry out to him day and night? Will he keep putting them off?*

3. Power And Wisdom To Overcome Temptations, Trials And Troubles That Characterize Our World.

Life is full of temptations, trials, challenges and obstacles. And they come on a daily basis. It seems that as we are coming out of one situation, another one is facing us. But thank God we have been assured of victory.

The Bible says:

When you pass through the waters, I will be with you; and when you pass through the rivers, they will not sweep over you. When you walk through the fire, you will not be burned; the flames will not set you ablaze. -

Isaiah 43:3:

It is only through a consistent and daily prayer life that we can generate the daily power and wisdom to win in these situations.

4. Daily Victory Over Satanic Plans And Attacks.

There are evil people all around us. There is a spiritual war going on against us. This is not just a spiritual hullaballoo. Satanic attacks and traps exist. Your victory over them depends on how you handle your prayer life.

1 Peter 5:8-9 (NIV)

Be alert and of sober mind. Your enemy the devil prowls around like a roaring lion looking for someone to devour.

Resist him, standing firm in the faith, because you know that the family of believers throughout the world is undergoing the same kind of sufferings.

We cannot gain spiritual and physical victory in life by simply muttering some kind of motivational gibberish daily and hope that that is all that is required to fulfill our destinies.

We need real practical and effective daily

praying to obtain victory in our lives and fulfill God's plans. The once-in-a-while praying Christian will always be a victim of demonic works and attacks.

---

5. Live In God's Presence

Dr. David Yongi Cho said,

"The more time you spend with God, the more of the Holy Spirit you will have."

The Psalmist said that he that dwells in the secret place of the Most High shall abide under the shadow of the Almighty (Psalm 91:1). God said to Moses, ***"My Presence will go with you, and I will give you***

rest.*"* (Exodus 33:14).

Beloved, the presence of God is the greatest secret of favor, peace and outstanding success. We must do whatever it takes to stay in His presence daily.

---

6. Grow Your Spiritual Gifts.

Your spiritual gifts will manifest more and more only as you practically develop an effective prayer life. Unfortunately, these days, the church no longer talk about gifts of the Spirit. We focus more on motivating our people. We tell them that if they can just give enough, we'll get on some other TV stations and win the lost for Jesus.

Imagine that.

And we wonder why we are not having revival.

Beloved, every child of God is expected to bear fruits for the Kingdom. We are expected to win souls, heal the sick, cast out devils, recognize the leading of the Spirit and cause great changes in our environments.

Jesus said:

"I am the true vine, and my Father is the gardener. He cuts off every branch in me

that bears no fruit, while every branch that

does bear fruit he prunes so that it will be

even more fruitful."- (John 15:2)

Prayer and the word of God are the food of the Spirit. As you regularly feed on them your spiritual gifts stirs up more and more and manifest.

Jesus is warning us in the above scripture that if we do not bear fruit, that we will be plucked out. Unfortunately there are many Christians who are already plucked out but don't know it. Because they are so busy with church activities, they think that everything is fine.

Beloved, God wants you to bear fruits.

---

7. Deal With Carnality.

I've come to a point in my life several times where I wonder why I'm this carnal. There seems to be a serious fight inside me to act the way I don't want. Like Apostle Paul, I keep wondering, why is it that what I want to do is not what I find myself doing (Romans 7:15). No matter how I take new decisions and form determination, I keep failing. It was until God began to show me that I can't overcome carnality if I don't address my personal prayer life that I began to see where the problem lies.

Whoever sows to please their flesh, from the flesh will reap destruction; whoever sows to please the Spirit, from the Spirit will reap eternal life. – Galatians 6:8

Carnality thrives in the absence of the spirit. We can pretend all we can before people but truth is that we have a lot of fights going on within. The only way to gain this inner victory is sowing daily into our spiritual lives through personal effective personal prayers.

8. Learn to Recognize The Voice Of God.

Almost every Christian is asking, *'how I can hear the voice of God?'* We seem to always be in a wonder state if God is really speaking to us. If He is speaking, what is He saying? How do we know He is the one speaking?

But the Bile says:

Hear, you deaf; look, you blind, and see!

Who is blind but my servant, and deaf like the messenger I send? Who is blind like the one in covenant with me, blind like the servant of the LORD?

You have seen many things, but you pay no

attention; your ears are open, but you do not listen." –Isaiah 42:18-20

This is a very powerful scripture that has made a lot of impact in my life. God is simply saying there that He is speaking, but we are not listening. He has said so many things to us, things that would have changed our lives for great good, but we are just too busy with our own stuff, that we are not seeing what He is saying.

The fault is not from God's side, but from us.

Beloved, I pray that you do not miss what God is telling you personally, as a result of being too busy, in Jesus name. If you want to be able to always recognize the voice of God, then address your personal daily prayer life.

You don't have to be among those who complain of not hearing the voice of God, who keep turning round and round in life, confused. We develop the ability to recognize the voice of God more and more if our prayer life is in order.

My sheep listen to my voice; I know them, and they follow me. - John 10:27

---

9. Prayer Is A Seed.

We often hear about give, give and give and most times our presumption about giving is that money is the only best thing we need to give. However, that's not right. Money is not the only thing we can give.

Prayer is a seed, a very great seed. In fact, prayer is the very best of all seeds that we can give to others because it will do for others what we cannot even do for them. This is a secret that can change your life.

I used to be worried when I don't have enough money to give and help people who come to me for help. Many times I would feel guilty when I am asked for help and I couldn't help much. But God has shown me that money is not the only thing we can give. When we sincerely pray for others from our hearts, we are sowing greater seeds than money.

For example, Abraham prayed earnestly for Lot and he was saved from destruction. That was certainly better than giving him money or possessions.

The men turned away and went toward Sodom, but Abraham remained standing before the Lord.

Then Abraham approached him and said:

"Will you sweep away the righteous with the wicked?

What if there are fifty righteous people in the city? Will you really sweep it away and not spare the place for the sake of the fifty righteous people in it?

Far be it from you to do such a thing—to kill the righteous with the wicked, treating the righteous and the wicked alike. Far be it from you! Will not the Judge of all the earth do right?"

The Lord said, "If I find fifty righteous people in the city of Sodom, I will spare the whole place for their sake."

Then Abraham spoke up again: "Now that I have been so bold as to speak to the Lord, though I am nothing but dust and ashes, what if the number of the righteous is five less than fifty? Will you destroy the whole city for lack of five people?"

"If I find forty-five there," he said, "I will not destroy it."

Once again he spoke to him, "What if only forty are found there?"

He said, "For the sake of forty, I will not do it."

Then he said, "May the Lord not be angry, but let me speak. What if only thirty can be found there?"

He answered, "I will not do it if I find thirty there."

Abraham said, "Now that I have been so bold as to speak to the Lord, what if only twenty can be found there?"

He said, "For the sake of twenty, I will not destroy it."

Then he said, "May the Lord not be angry, but let me speak just once more. What if only ten can be found there?"

He answered, "For the sake of ten, I will not destroy it." - **Gen 18: 22- 32,**

Abraham simply kept praying until Lot was spared from the destruction of Sodom and Gomorrah.

Beloved, if you are always worried that you can't help enough, worry no more. By sincerely praying for others, you are giving much more than money. Prayer is a very powerful seed that will be multiplied back to into your life.

Call people's names in your prayers, especially in your private prayers. By that way you are sowing greater seeds. God will cause others to pray for you and cause the things you pray to happen for others to happen in your own life as well.

---

10. Jesus, the Son Of God Prayed Daily

If Jesus, the son of God, needed to pray effectively everyday while here on earth to fulfill his assignment, then we surely need prayer to achieve anything worthwhile here.

Jesus began with prayer, grew with prayer, worked with prayer and ended with prayer. He never took any major decision or performed an extraordinary miracle without serious prayers preceding.

Before he walked on the sea he spent more than six hours in personal prayer (Matt.

14:22-27). He spent several hours in prayer before he received grace to face the cross (luke.22:39-46).

Prayer is the backbone of any successful ministry.

There is no way we can achieve those wonderful dreams of greatness in our hearts without the backing of spiritual power, because life is a battle field. No matter how hard we try, when there is no supernatural power backing us, we'll only be struggling.

"I have seen something else under the sun: The race is not to the swift or the battle to the strong, nor does food come to the wise or

*wealth to the brilliant or favor to the learned; but time and chance happen to them all."– **Ecclesiastes 9:11***

I believe that we cannot do much for God in our lives without an effective prayer life.

Chapter 2: It's Easier Than You Thought: 10 Practical Suggestions For Building A Powerful Prayer Life.

1. Decide.

Sometimes we tend to think that God is the one who gains when we pray. Fortunately, it is we who gain much more. Everything revolves around helping us become better and achieve better fulfillment, both in the workplace and in the family.

Beloved, God wants to have more intimacy with you daily. This intimacy will help you the more. It will give you better insight into how our world operates and position you for daily victory in life.

To answer this call begins with a decision. You have to say inside of you, "LORD, here are am I! Help me"

When you make this decision, you'll realize that the Holy Spirit will help you. You'll begin to see that you can actually have more time for this personal spiritual fellowship.

I have noticed that there are one thousand and one things willing to keep us away from praying: social media, TV, children, health, neighbors, etc.

You know why these things want to stop us?

That's because prayer works. ***Prayer is the smallest part that handles the biggest issues of our lives.*** That is why those issues want to keep us away from it.

Personally decide that nothing will hinder your daily prayers from today. Without this kind decision and determination you will remain where you are.

Many times, in fact almost all the time, you won't feel like praying. The push to pray may not be there. You may feel very tired and exhausted and only want to sleep. Your daily involvement might even tend to justify your need to stay away from prayer. However, you must stand by your decision and discipline yourself. You must push yourself to pray. As you begin and continue then the Holy Spirit will come to help you.

---

2. Map Out Time.

Next is to map out a prayer time. Don't worry; you may not always keep this time because things will always come up. You may travel out of town or have a prayer night in the church or anything. But it's good to still map out a specific time for your personal prayers.

Is it going to be between 5:00am to 5:45am?

Choose a specific time you think may be convenient for you and commit this time to God in prayer. Ask God for His power to keep up with this covenant time.

---

3. Awareness.

Inform other members of your family about this time. It may be that in some instances one member of the family might remind you about it.

---

4. Make a List.

Make a list of areas that needs prayer coverage in your family, church and neighborhood. Those who need to be saved, those who need to be baptized with the Holy Spirit, those who need business breakthrough, those who need deliverance and divine intervention. I assure you, you won't be able to pray through the list in each personal prayer session.

But you can always continue where you stopped next time. The essence of this list is to help you know when God has answered your prayer and you can mark the point as done. As you do, watch your faith as it increases.

Note that no one may know that you are

doing the prayer for those people. But God who sees in secret and rewards openly has assured you that you will not lose your rewards.

---

5. Discipline.

Discipline yourself to be regular with the time you have mapped out for personal prayers. Remember that issues will always come up. When you fail, don't feel guilty but try to get back to your covenant time special.

I discipline my body like an athlete, training it to do what it should. Otherwise, I fear that after preaching to others I myself might be

6. Offer to Pray With Others.

To improve your prayer life is a goal that must be achieved with everything you've got. Occasionally offer prayer assistance for others. There are instances when I've asked people, friends and colleagues at times, if I could join them in prayer; or if there are things they need to be prayed for. When I'm given some, I start praying right away. I don't really wait to pray specially. I just start talking to God and pleading for His intervention.

7. Don't Feel You are Not Praying Well.

Those who claim to be teaching about prayer often times want to confuse us. They give us so many lectures that we now tend to think that there are prayers that God doesn't attend to. For me, I have learned that I can pray to God, anyway, anyhow. There is no specific method. So don't think that if you don't shout, that you haven't prayed well; or that you must pray in a certain way to be sure that you have really prayed. The scripture says:

And pray in the Spirit on all occasions with all kinds of prayers and requests. With this in mind, be alert and always keep on praying for all the Lord's people. – Ephesians 6:18.

---

8. Practice Praying Anytime, Anywhere.

Someone may ask, is the prayer we say in church more powerful than the ones we say in our hearts while driving or in the office?

Honestly, I don't think so.

Like I said above, God has helped me to understand that I can pray anywhere, anyhow, anytime. Talking to God in my heart even in the midst of my **busyness** has helped me to draw closer to God more than I could think of. This type of prayer is very good and it's one great way to build your personal prayer life despite the tight schedules. Remember what the scripture says:

Now unto him that is able to do exceeding abundantly above all that we ask or think, according to the power that worketh in us. - **Ephesians 3:20**.

There is the thinking part which the Bible also recognizes as prayer; meaning that we can daily draw closer to God through praying in our thoughts, even while busy with other stuff.

---

9. Pray With a Note.

Whenever you go to have your personal prayers, try to go with a prayer note. If you feel led to read a particular passage of the Bible, write it down. If you feel God is laying an idea in your heart, write it down. Don't trust your memory to remember everything later on. Believe me, years to come, you will look at this prayer note and give God praise for it.

Real prayer is not a one way affair. When we talk to God, we can expect that He will talk back to us. That is the best form of prayer. It's called fellowship with God.

---

10. Seek the Lord in Fasting Once in a While.

I know there are different kinds of fasting when we talk about the practice of fasting, but I want to talk about something else. I want to talk about fasting because you are led in your heart by God to fast, and fasting because you just want to fast. Both types of fasting are very necessary. In fact, to be able to grow a powerful personal prayer life, practice the act of fasting once in a while, on your own. It may be once in a week, or once in a month, or whatever.

Every Christian should have a particular day personally set apart for seeking the face of God in fasting and praying. This is one way to invoke constant fresh ideas and revelation from heaven to push through in life.

Please note the following about fasting:

- Do not embark on a fasting that will hurt your body. The first time I fasted, it was 6:00am - 10:00am. Till today, I still do all manner of fasts. I fast 6PM-6AM; I can skip lunch to pray, etc. The major purpose of fasting is to read the Bible and pray. Let's not get it twisted. Learn to start small and add as you grow.

- I don't normally feel guilty drinking water whenever I am fasting because it helps give me the strength to pray; but if you don't like the idea don't worry about it.

- Write out on paper the burning issues of your heart that recently evolved around you which you will tell God during your fasting day. If you think you don't have much to pray about, then pray for others.

Chapter 3: Simple But Effective Prayer Outline That Can Help You During Personal Prayers and Devotions.

Below are prayer outlines that can help you spend more time with God in prayer. Remember that this is just a personal prayer outline. You may not follow it. It's just to give you an idea.

45 Minutes Personal Prayer Outline.

ITEM	TIME
Praise and worship	5 Mins
Thanksgiving prayer	5 mins
Prayer for the Holy Spirit	5 mins

Empowerment	
Reading and Meditating on the Word	15 mins
Binding every power of Satan against your life and family.	5 mins
Making intercession for others by calling names and praying	10 Mins
Total time spent = 45 Mins	

1 Hour Personal Prayer Outline.

ITEM	TIME
Praise and worship	5 Mins
Thanksgiving prayer	5 mins
Prayer for the Holy Spirit Empowerment	5 mins
Reading and Meditating on the Word	30 mins
Binding every power of Satan against your life and family.	5 mins
Making intercession for others by calling names and praying	10 Mins
Total time spent = 60 Mins	

Note: Like I said, this is just an outline. As you make use of this outline the Holy Spirit will fill your heart with some prayer points. Pray them. Sometimes you'll see yourself praying more than the time apportioned, that's great.

Chapter 4: Tips For Effective Bible Study During Personal Prayers and Devotions.

If you look at the prayer outlines above you'll notice that we have made sure there is time for bible reading and meditation. That's because I strongly believe that ***our spiritual growth is not all about how much we talk to God, but how much God talks to us that we understand and follow.***

So in order to get the best out of your personal Bible reading times, let's talk about few steps that have helped me.

1. Exercise Book:

I cannot over emphasize this enough. You need to have a personal prayer and study note. This is very important. I call mine **"Daily Inspiration"** exercise book. You need this to have a great Bible study experience in your personal prayer.

2. Preplan:

Before your prayer times, decide the chapter you will study beforehand. You may be reading on a particular scriptural subject or character and wish to continue with it during your devotion, that's great. The point is to know what you want to read beforehand.

3. Make Notes:

Write the day's date on the page in your "Daily Inspirations" note book, time and the chapter or book or subject you are studying. Look at the example below:

DATE	MONDAY (29/09/13)
TIME OF STUDY	5: 00AM – 5: 45AM
BOOK OF STUDY	Isaiah 53: 1 -5
INSPIRATIONS	

Then as you study the particular chapter or book or subject write whatever idea or thought that comes into your mind.

4. Use Questions To Help Stretch Your Mind:

Whatever you are reading on, ask yourself:

1. What is the verse saying about God?

2. What is the passage saying about Christ?

3. What is the passage saying about the Holy Spirit?

4. What does God expect me to do with these verses and lessons?

Write down every impression. Years later, you will look back and thank God you did.

5. Prayer:

Spend a few minutes and pray the scripture you just read and ask God to make the lessons real in your life.

Chapter 5: Tips To Overcome Body Weakness During Personal Prayer And Bible Study Times.

As I said before, ninety percent of the time you won't feel like praying. I am talking from my own personal experience. However, God has made me realize that prayer is not what we have to wait until we feel like doing it before we can do it. We just have to pray.

We just have to start praying. As you start, your feeling will take care of itself. Tell the Holy Spirit to help you, and as you proceed He will quicken your body.

If you are waiting until the feeling comes, you

will never pray. Remember, the Holy Spirit won't do the praying. You will start it, and then He comes to help.

To help yourself of being carried away by sleep while praying or reading the Word of God, do not overeat before going to prayer or personal study. That will make you very weak and sleep off. You can also do some exercise to properly arouse your body. And if you know that when you kneel or lie down to pray or study that you may feel sleepy, then stand or move around and pray and study.

However, there are other times you will naturally feel very weak. Maybe you've really overworked during the day or whatever. Those times even when you stand you'll feel like you'll fall. At such times try as much as you can to say some prayers before resting.

As you fall back to have some rest ask the Holy Spirit to quicken you at a particular time. He normally does.

Remember, the one who sow to please his body will reap destruction, but the one who sow to please his spirit will reap eternal joy (Galatians 5: 8)

If you want to win in the affairs of life every day, then train yourself, discipline yourself, and work on yourself, to have a strong prayer life. Use the secrets provided in this book and see your relationship with God grow.

Other Books from the Author.

1. <u>Prayer Retreat:</u> 500 Powerful Prayers & Declarations to Destroy Stubborn Demonic Problems, Dislodge Every Spiritual Wickedness Against Your Life and Release Your Detained Blessings

2. <u>HEALING PRAYERS & CONFESSIONS:</u> Powerful Daily Meditations, Prayers and Declarations for Total Healing and Divine Health.

3. <u>200 Violent Prayers</u> for Deliverance, Healing and Financial Breakthrough.

4. <u>Hearing God's Voice in Painful Moments:</u> 21 Days Bible Meditations and Prayers to Bring Comfort, Strength and Healing When Grieving for the Loss of

Someone You Love.

5 . Healing Prayers: 30 Powerful Prophetic Prayers that Brings Healing and Empower You to Walk in Divine Health.

6. Healing WORDS: 55 Powerful Daily Confessions & Declarations to Activate Your Healing & Walk in Divine Health: Strong Decrees That Invoke Healing for You & Your Loved Ones

7. Prayers That Break Curses and Spells and Release Favors and Breakthroughs.

8. 7 Days Fasting With 120 Powerful Night Prayers for Personal Deliverance and Breakthrough.

9. 100 Powerful Prayers for Your Teenagers: Powerful Promises and Prayers to Let God Take Control of Your Teenagers & Get Them to

Experience Love & Fulfillment

14. How to Cast Out Demons from Your Home, Office and Property: 100 Powerful Prayers to Cleanse Your Home, Office, Land & Property from Demonic Attacks

15. Praying Through the Book of Psalms: Most Powerful Psalms and Powerful Prayers & Declarations for Every Situation: Birthday, Christmas, Business Ideas, Breakthrough, Deliverance, Healing, Comfort, Exams, Decision Making, Grief, and Many More.

16. STUDENTS' PRAYER BOOK: Powerful Motivation & Guide for Students & Anyone Preparing to Write Exams: Plus 10 Days of Powerful Prayers for Wisdom, Favor, Protection & Success in Studies, Exams & Life.

17. How to Pray and Receive Financial Miracle

Let Us Hear from You.

We love testimonies. We love to hear what God is doing around the world as people draw close to Him in prayer. Please share your story with us.

Also, please consider giving this book a review on Amazon and checking out our other titles at:

amazon.com/author/danielokpara

I also invite you to checkout our website at www.BetterLifeWorld.org and consider joining our newsletter, which we send out once in a while with great tips, testimonies and revelations from God's Word for a victorious living.

Feel free to <u>drop us your prayer request</u>. We will join faith with you and God's power will be released in your life and the issue in question.

About the Author.

Daniel Okpara brings you the message of hope, healing, deliverance and total restoration. A humble minister and teacher of God's Word, businessman and lecturer, he is a strong believer that with God all things are possible.

Yes. The challenges of life are real, but with faith, you will surely win. Your health, relationship, and finances can be restored by God's grace and power, no matter how bad things are at the moment.

He is the international director of Better Life

World Outreach Center, a non-denominational, evangelism based ministry with commitment to:

- Taking the entire Gospel to the entire world, from village to village, town to town, city to city, state to state and nation to nation, in partnership with established churches.

- Training ministers, evangelists and missionaries and providing them with tools, resources and impartation for the end-time assignment.

- Restoring the evangelism fire in the body of Christ through church workers' revivals and trainings.

- Producing evangelism materials and tools (films, tracts, books, devotionals) for rural, screen and world evangelism.

He is the host of Better Life Today, a Monthly non-denominational fellowship meeting where hundreds of people gather for business workshops, worship, healing, miracles and diverse encounters with God. He also co-hosts a popular radio and TV program, "**Keys to a Better Life**", aired in over 10 radio and TV stations across the country.

Daniel Okpara holds a Master's Degree in Theology from Cornerstone Christian University. As a strong believer in hard work, continuous learning and prosperity by value creation, he is also the founder of Integrity Assets Ltd, a real estate and IT consulting company that manages an eCommerce startup and consults for companies on Digital Marketing.

He has authored over 50 books and manuals on healing, prayer, Marriage and relationship, Investment, Doing business and Digital Marketing.

He is married to Prophetess Doris Okpara, a prayer warrior and great support and they are blessed with a boy and a girl, Isaac and Annabel.

35835572R00045

Printed in Poland
by Amazon Fulfillment
Poland Sp. z o.o., Wrocław